The KidHaven Science Library

Germs

by Don Nardo

KidHaven Press

KidHaven Press, an imprint of Gale Group, Inc.

10911 Technology Place, San Diego, CA 92127

On cover: Laboratory technicians examine bacteria colonies.

Library of Congress Cataloging-in-Publication Data
Nardo, Don, 1947–
  Germs / by Don Nardo.
     p. cm. — (the kidhaven science library)
  Summary: Describes different kinds of microorganisms, including bacteria, fungi, and algae, and both their harmful and beneficial effects, as well as efforts to prevent the harm that some germs cause.
  ISBN 0-7377-0943-X (hbk. : alk. paper)
  1. Microbiology—Juvenile literature. [1. Microbiology. 2. Microorganisms.] I. Title. II. Series.
QR57 .N368 2002
579—dc21

2001002787

Contents

Chapter 1
Germs Are Everywhere 4

Chapter 2
Fighting Germs That Cause Disease 14

Chapter 3
Identifying Helpful Germs 24

Chapter 4
Some Modern Uses for Germs 33

Glossary 42

For Further Exploration 44

Index 45

Picture Credits 47

About the Author 48

Germs Are Everywhere

Germs are very tiny living things. They are so small that people cannot see them with their eyes alone. Only by looking in a microscope, which makes things look bigger than they are, can someone see germs.

Germs are not only very tiny, they are numerous as well. Millions, and in some cases billions or trillions of germs, can fit in a teaspoon or a thimble. They are also everywhere. Germs exist in the air people breathe, in the food they eat, and in the water they drink. Germs are also found in soil and even on and inside the human body.

Some germs are harmful. They cause diseases, such as measles, chicken pox, sleeping sickness, lyme disease, and AIDS. Harmful germs can pass from animal to animal and person to person. So they sometimes cause large outbreaks of disease, called **epidemics**.

However, most germs are not dangerous. They play important roles in nature and have no harmful effects on animals and humans. Some of these germs are even helpful because they work to keep the body healthy.

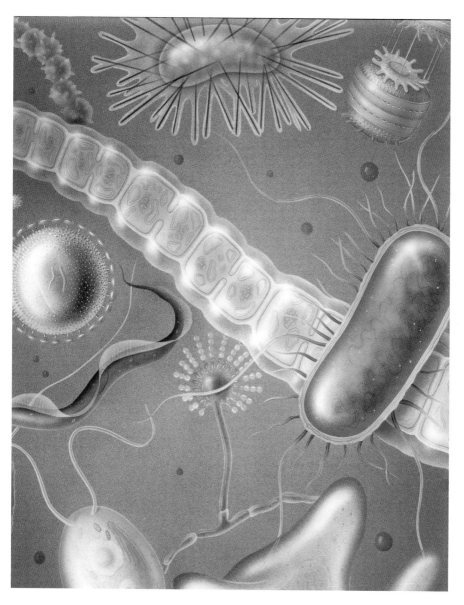

An artist's view of different kinds of germs.

Bacteria

Scientists first saw germs in the 1600s when the microscope was invented. Since that time, they have identified many thousands of different kinds of germs. Each has a certain shape and behavior. Still, some kinds of germs have fairly similar shapes and behaviors. So experts divide them into five basic groups. Each group consists of germs that look and act roughly the same.

One group is made up of germs called **bacteria**. Bacteria have very simple forms. Each bacterium consists of a single cell. Bacteria cells are so small that 30 trillion of them weigh a single ounce. Bacteria come in three main shapes: round, like balls; longer and thinner, like rods or tubes; and wavy or coiled.

However they may look, most bacteria **reproduce** in the same way. Each bacterium divides in half resulting in two germs that are exact copies of each other. The amount of time it takes for a new bacterium to begin to divide varies from one type to another. But the average is about twenty minutes. So, it would take only twenty minutes for one bacterium to divide into two, an hour for two to become eight, three hours to become 512, six hours to reach half a million, and nine hours to grow to 256 million.

This amazing rate of reproduction makes it very hard to wipe out any one kind of bacteria.

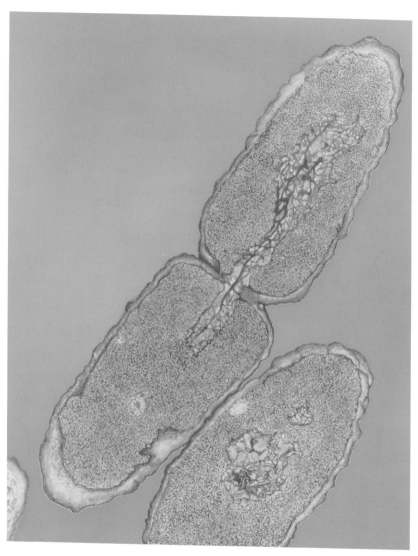

A bacterium reproduces by dividing in half.

Even if only a single bacterium survives, it can create trillions of its kind in less than a day. Also, many kinds of bacteria are very hardy, so they can survive harsh conditions that would kill most other living things. Bacteria have been found living in frozen soil, high in the sky where there is almost no air, and in hot springs where the water is boiling.

Fungi

A second group of germs, **fungi**, are also very numerous and hardy. There are also different kinds of fungi, and not all are germs. Mushrooms are a type of fungi, but they are not germs. Only microscopic fungi are classified as germs. These germs are too small to see with the eye, but they are larger than bacteria. A typical microscopic fungus is eight to twenty times the size of an average bacterium.

Microscopic fungi come in a wide variety of shapes. In general, though, most look a lot like small plants or like chains or strings of tiny beads. Microscopic fungi cannot make their own food, so they live on rotting matter such as dead leaves, dead animals, or old bread and fruit.

Most microscopic fungi reproduce by releasing tiny particles called **spores**. Wind and water spread the spores far and wide, and each grows into a new fungal cell.

One common kind of microscopic fungi is yeast. An average yeast cell is oval shaped. Three thousand such cells placed side by side would stretch about an inch. Some yeasts live on the skin or in the stomachs of warm-blooded ani-

A magnified view of fungi that live on the surface of rotting bread.

mals. Other yeasts cause bread to rise and grape juice to turn into wine. Still other yeasts cause painful infections in animals and humans.

Algae and Protozoa

Like fungi, **algae** come in many forms and sizes. Some kinds of algae consist of many cells and are several feet long. Only microscopic, one-celled algae can be classified as germs.

Most algae live in ponds or oceans (though some live in the soil). They take in sunlight and

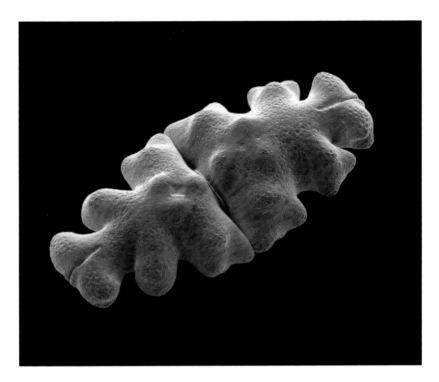

A close-up photo, taken with a microscope, shows a cell of green algae.

carbon dioxide, a common gas found in the air. An algae cell combines these two products for its food. Then it gives off another gas, oxygen, as a waste product. This process is important to animals and humans because they must breathe in oxygen to live. Algae are also a food source for larger organisms, especially fish. Most algae do not cause disease, but some can be poisonous to animals and people.

Water is also home to a fourth group of germs: **protozoa**. A few kinds of protozoa are as small as yeasts. But many are bigger, some so large that they are almost visible to the human eye. These are the largest of all germs.

Because they are so big, protozoa have room for a few simple internal, organlike parts. The largest

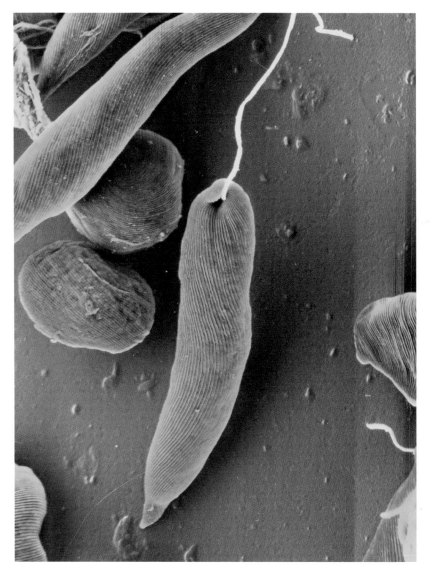

Protozoa like these are the largest kinds of germs.

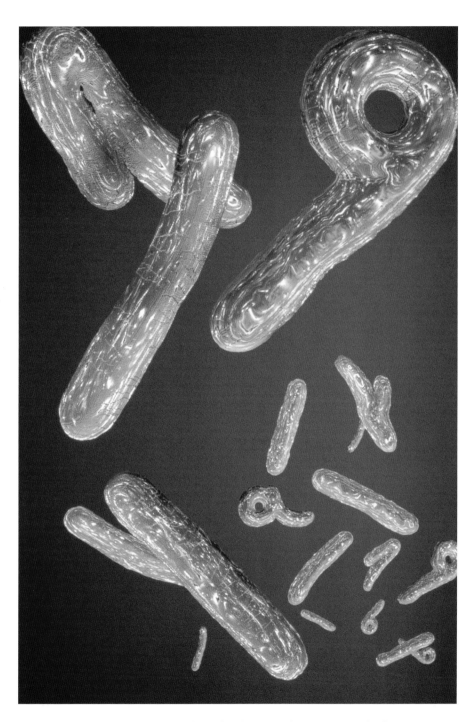

These viruses cause a deadly disease known as ebola.

Germs

is the nucleus, in the center. A protozoan repro-duces by splitting its nucleus in half, each half becoming the nucleus of a new germ. Protozoa often find homes in the moist bodies of animals and humans. These germs can cause harmful dis-eases such as malaria and sleeping sickness.

Viruses

While protozoa are the largest germs, the fifth kind—**viruses**—are the smallest. Viruses are hun-dreds, and in some cases thousands, of times smaller than bacteria. Viruses are so tiny that only the most powerful microscopes in the world can detect them. Most of these germs look like tiny rods twisted around many times like a corkscrew or spring (although they do come in other shapes).

Viruses cannot live long on their own. They sur-vive by invading and living inside a cell of a plant or animal. Once inside the host cell, a virus uses the materials it finds there to make new viruses. A single viral germ can multiply into hundreds or even thousands of viruses. These then invade other nearby cells.

Some viruses are harmless to animals and peo-ple. But many viruses, like some bacteria, fungi, and protozoa, cause serious diseases. Doctors and other scientists constantly struggle to cure or stop the spread of these diseases.

Chapter 2

Fighting Germs That Cause Disease

Germs that are harmful to animals and humans, especially germs that spread diseases, have caused much misery throughout the ages. Bubonic plague, known as the "Black Death," wiped out millions of people in the 1300s. The germ that caused the plague was a bacterium carried by fleas. In the early 1900s, some 20 million people worldwide died of another dreaded disease called influenza. This time the culprit was a virus. In those same years, hundreds of thousands of people in Africa lost their lives to a protozoan disease—sleeping sickness.

Beginning in the 1800s, modern doctors and scientists made great strides in fighting such deadly diseases. To do so, they followed a series of steps, which is still followed today. The first step is to identify the kind of germ causing the disease. The second step is to find out how the germ makes people sick. Next, the doctors search for a cure, or if no cure can be found, they look for a way to relieve suffering.

Citizens of the Congo, in Africa, line up to receive shots to protect them from sleeping sickness in the 1920s.

One other important step—maybe the most important—is to find a way to keep the disease from spreading. The doctors who track down the source of a deadly disease are known as **epidemiologists**, or sometimes "disease detectives."

How Germs Cause Disease

The first step in fighting diseases—identifying the germs that cause them—is the easiest one. Today, labs around the world are equipped with powerful microscopes and other tools. These tools allow doctors to determine if an illness is caused by bacteria, fungi, protozoa, or viruses.

A scientist uses a microscope to identify the germs that cause disease.

The second step—figuring out how these germs cause disease—is harder. In the last one hundred years, experts have learned how most harmful germs attack the body. Like viruses, most other disease germs invade the blood or cells of an animal or human. Once inside the body, some germs find what they need in the blood. Others bore into and feed off of the cells.

However they obtain food, disease germs give off waste materials or other substances. These substances, called toxins, are poisonous. They can cause fever, headaches, and vomiting. They can also weaken the heart and other organs. People who contract sleeping sickness, for example, suffer from fever, headaches, and chills at first. Then they begin to feel weak and sleepy until their bodies give out and they die.

Helping the Body Fight Invaders

Germs that cause illness do not always cause death. In many cases, after only a few days or maybe a couple of weeks, the illness goes away. This usually happens with the common cold. Most colds go away by themselves. This is because the body has its own natural forces for fighting harmful germs. When the body detects harmful germs, it rushes special germ-fighting agents to the site. Some of these agents are tiny particles called **antibodies**. The antibodies attach themselves to and cover an invading germ. That keeps the germ from reproducing and spreading. The body also sends in large cells that feed on some of the attacking germs.

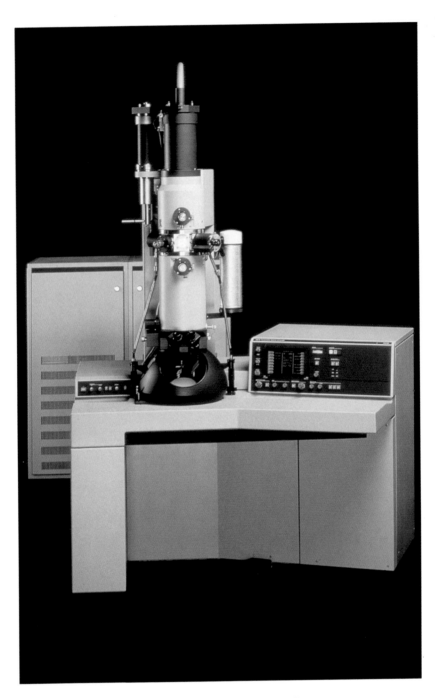

The powerful electron microscope, seen here, can even detect viruses.

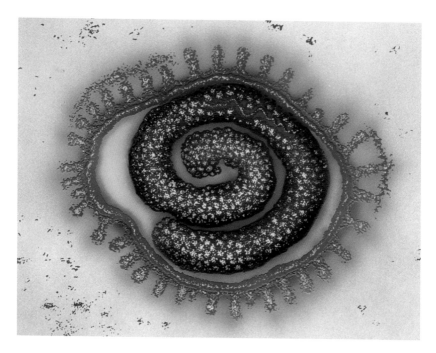

An electron microscope image shows viruses invading a living cell.

Doctors have learned to take advantage of these natural healing forces by making them stronger. This is the idea behind vaccines, one of the best weapons used to fight diseases caused by germs. A vaccine is made up of a few disease germs that doctors have made weaker in the lab. A doctor injects the vaccine into the body of a healthy person. Immediately, the body's germ-fighting forces go to work and destroy the invaders. In the process, those forces learn to recognize the particular kind of germ involved. If the germs of that same disease invade again later on, the body's forces attack them much quicker and

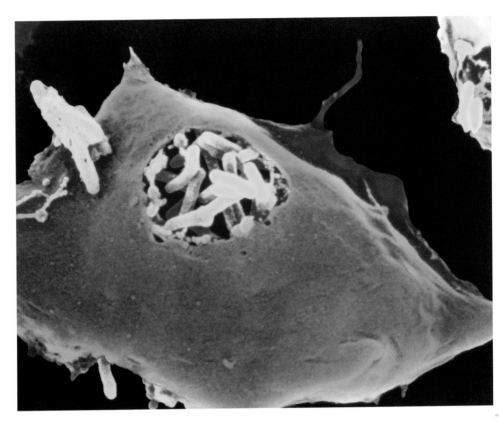

One of the body's germ-fighting cells swallows invading bacteria.

more forcefully. In this way, the disease usually can no longer harm the vaccinated person.

Unfortunately, vaccines have not yet been developed for all diseases. Also, in many parts of the world, large numbers of people do not use the vaccines that *have* been developed. Often, this is because they are very poor and cannot afford medical care. Or their governments do not provide enough doctors and vaccines. Even in rich countries such as the United States, some people do not get vaccinated. So, disease epidemics remain a threat.

Disease Detectives at Work

Where vaccines cannot stop a disease from spreading, sometimes disease detectives can. They study how diseases spread and find ways to control outbreaks before they become epidemics. Sometimes they can keep a disease from spreading without the use of medicine.

This is what happened in Africa in the early 1900s. British disease detectives wanted to find a way to slow or halt the spread of sleeping sickness. This terrible disease killed about 200,000 people in the country of Uganda in a period of only seven years. The disease claimed thousands of people in other African nations as well.

After a careful search of the countryside and some brilliant detective work, the doctors made an important discovery. They found that sleeping sickness was caused by a protozoan. These large germs lived in the local lakes and rivers. Flies laid their eggs in the water, where the germs infected them. When the new flies hatched and matured, they carried the germs to nearby villages. There, the insects bit humans. And the sleeping sickness germs passed through the tiny bite wounds and entered the people's bloodstreams.

After hearing about this discovery, local officials asked the villagers to move their homes farther away from rivers and lakes. The idea was to reduce the amount of contact between flies and humans. Many villagers agreed to move. Sure enough, in

Medical researchers examine slides containing samples of deadly diseases.

The protozoa that causes sleeping sickness infects the larvae of flies like this one.

only a few years, the number of cases of sleeping sickness in Uganda dropped dramatically.

Unfortunately, the protozoa that cause the illness are still in the local waters. And many of the flies in the area still carry these germs. So, some new cases of sleeping sickness occur each year. But thanks to hardworking doctors and scientists, this disease and many others caused by germs no longer kill thousands or millions of people.

Chapter 3

Identifying Helpful Germs

Not all germs are dangerous or destructive. Only a small number of germs cause diseases. Many bacteria, fungi, and other germs are harmless. In fact, most germs are helpful to plants, animals, and humans. Certain kinds of germs keep living things healthy and help them function normally. Moreover, many kinds of germs play important roles in nature. The daily and yearly cycles of life and death on earth depend on these helpful germs.

Germs at Work in Nature

One of the most important jobs germs have in nature is to help plants nourish themselves. Green plants need nitrogen to live. Nitrogen is the most plentiful gas in the planet's air. Certain germs found in soil help plants take in nitrogen from the air.

These same germs help animals and humans, too. Both animals and people eat plants. And

Some germs help plants nourish themselves by taking in nitrogen from the air.

most people eat animals and animal products such as milk, eggs, and cheese. So animals and humans depend on the germs that help plants process nitrogen just as much as plants do.

Other germs, especially algae, make oxygen. Much of the oxygen that animals and plants breathe every minute of every day comes from algae. So without these helpful germs, insects, reptiles, dogs, cats, horses, and people could not live.

Algae and other germs in the oceans play another vital role in nature. They form the base, or bottom, of nature's food chain. These germs take in sunlight and the gas carbon dioxide, as well as nutrients from the water. Tiny animals in the water then eat the germs. These small creatures, in turn, become the food for larger animals, especially fish. In the final link in the chain, humans, bears, and other more complex animals eat the fish.

The Role of Germs in Death

Just as germs help create and sustain life, they also play an important role in death. All forms of life eventually die, and nature must constantly remove and recycle dead plants and animals to make way for new ones. Many germs, particularly bacteria and fungi, help in this process. These germs actually live by eating the remains of dead plants and animals. They also release substances that make the remains decay, or break down into

Bears eat fish, which eat smaller creatures, which in their turn eat algae, and other germs.

simpler elements. These basic elements, such as carbon and nitrogen, then become part of the soil and air. Finally, new plants take in the carbon, nitrogen, and other elements. They use these elements to build their tissues. Animals and people then eat the plants to build their own tissues. And the cycle of life and death, aided by germs in each step, repeats itself.

Our Bodies Crawl with Germs

With so many germs in the air, soil, and water, it is not surprising that germs exist on animals and people, too. Every healthy person has trillions of harmless germs on and in his or her body. Some of these germs are found on the skin. Scientists estimate that about 30 million germs exist on a piece of skin the size of a postage stamp. Even more germs live inside the body.

Some of these harmless germs live on the millions of dead cells the body casts off every day. Unlike disease germs, which attack the body's cells, many of these harmless germs keep the body running properly. Others eat various other waste materials the body produces. Some of these

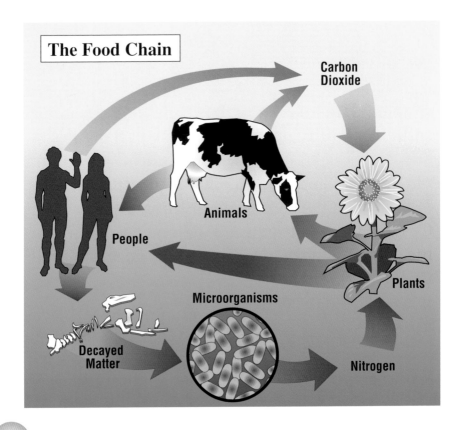

The Food Chain

Carbon Dioxide

Animals

People

Plants

Microorganisms

Decayed Matter

Nitrogen

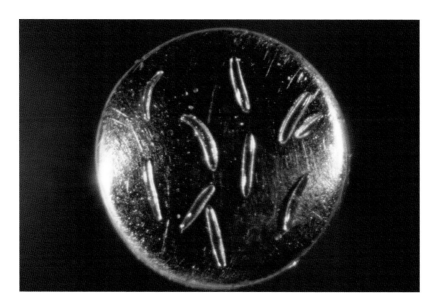

Bacteria, seen on the head of a pin, live inside human intestines and aid in digestion.

germs are very specialized. That means that they live only in certain parts of the body such as the mouth or the intestines.

Helping to Digest Food and Pump Blood

Germs in the intestines, for example, help animals and humans digest their food. They do this first by ensuring that the intestines develop normally. To digest food properly, the walls of the intestines must have a certain thickness. The walls must also be strong enough to squeeze together and push the food along. Experts admit they are not sure how and why germs help the

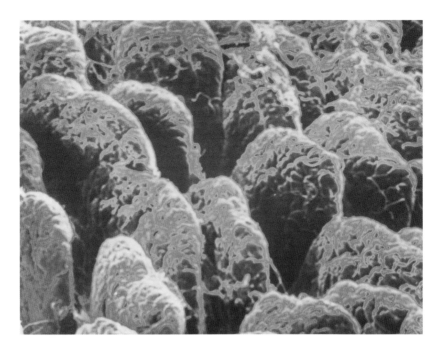

Germs aid development of the thick, healthy folds lining the inside of the human intestines.

intestines to grow normally. But a number of experiments have proven that this occurs.

In one such experiment, researchers raised guinea pigs in a germ-free area. The intestines of these animals grew much too thin. They were too weak to move food along properly, so the animals died. The scientists then fed bacteria normally found in animals' intestines to some germ-free guinea pigs. Within only a few weeks, their intestines grew thicker and stronger. And these animals lived normal, healthy lives.

Other organs besides the intestines require the help of germs to run normally. The heart, which pumps blood through the body, is an important example. Certain germs that live on and in the heart affect the amount of blood it can pump. Tests have shown that without these special

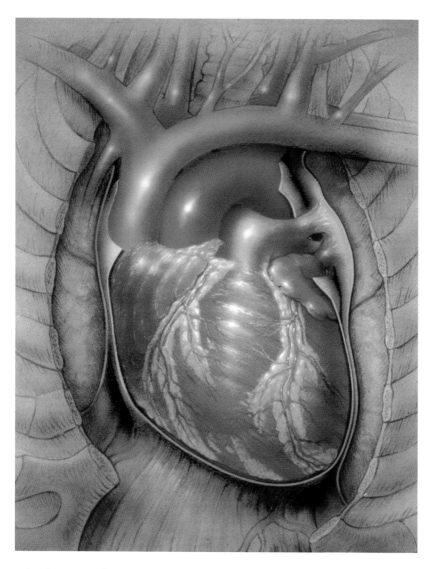

The human heart pumps blood through the body with the help of germs.

germs, the heart pumps less blood, which is harmful to a person's health.

Germs That Make Vitamins

Another way that germs aid the body is by helping it make many of the vitamins it needs. Vitamins are tiny substances that keep the body healthy. Vitamin A, for example, helps the bones and teeth develop properly. Various B vitamins aid in digesting the fats that animals and people take in when they eat. Certain B vitamins also help make red blood cells, which carry oxygen throughout the body. Without the right amounts of certain vitamins, a person will become weak and sick. In extreme cases, a lack of these vitamins can even cause death.

A large number of vitamins in the body are made by bacteria. When food passes into the intestines, the bacteria go to work changing food into vitamins. The body then absorbs these vitamins and uses them in many ways.

People and germs have a special relationship. People give germs a place to live and thrive. And in return, these tiny living things make it possible for *people* to live and thrive.

Some Modern Uses for Germs

Germs benefit modern life in many surprising ways. They add variety to the foods people eat. They help keep communities and the environment clean. They even help farmers combat pests that threaten to destroy crops.

Although germs are one cause of spoilage in food, some foods are made with the help of germs. When yeasts multiply in grape juice, for example, the juice sours and becomes wine.

In a like manner, certain kinds of bacteria cause milk to sour. After a while, the sour milk becomes lumpy. The lumps are called curd, which people have long used to make cheese. Some types of cheese are sold and eaten right away before they ripen, or age. These include cream cheese and ricotta cheese. Other cheeses are aged. During the aging process, bacteria in the cheese release substances that give the cheese its flavor. Other foods and drinks that require bacteria or fungi include bread, yogurt, beer, vinegar, pickles, olives, and soy sauce.

During the process of aging, germs release chemicals that give cheese its flavor.

Once scientists understood how to affect certain foods, food makers could use that knowledge to control food production. They learned to add just the right amounts of various germs to cheese and other foods to get the desired flavors or textures.

People have also learned to use germs in other practical ways. Industry, farms, and communities all benefit from putting germs to work. These make people's lives easier, cleaner, and safer.

Germs in Sewage Treatment

One of the most effective modern uses for germs is treating sewage. Sewage is the mixture of liquid and solid wastes that people discard each day. Most people flush these wastes down the toilet and forget about them. But the solid parts, called **sludge**, build up quickly. People everywhere used to dump the sludge in the ground, or more often into rivers and oceans. Many cities in many countries still use this method. However, scientists have shown that dumping sludge into the water pollutes it. It kills some of the animals that live in the water and makes the water unsafe for people to fish or swim in it.

Most large cities in the United States have solved this problem by using germs to eliminate sludge. This modern method of sewage treatment begins by separating the liquid wastes from the solid ones. Workers pump the raw sewage into large open tanks. In the course of a few hours, the solid materials slowly settle to the bottom. Next, the workers put the sludge in special tanks containing bacteria that thrive on such wastes. The germs digest the sludge. And as they do so, they

Workers at a sewage treatment plant inspect a tank containing sludge.

break it down into simpler materials that are not harmful to animals and people.

Sewage treatment plants receive an added bonus from this process. One of the materials the germs create while eating the sludge is a gas called methane. Methane burns easily, so it can be used as a fuel. The workers collect the methane made by the germs and use the gas to power the plant's machines.

Fighting "Bad" Insects

Both farms and towns benefit from another creative use of germs—fighting insect pests. Some insects, including mosquitoes and flies, carry diseases. Other insects seriously damage crops every year in all corners of the globe. Scientists have searched long and hard for ways to control these pests. They developed poisons to spray crops and ponds where insects lay their eggs. These poisons kill the insects, but they also pollute the soil and water, which poses a danger to people and animals.

As a result, many farmers and pest control experts have turned to certain kinds of bacteria to kill "bad" insects. Like all germs, these bacteria release substances when they reproduce. The substances these germs give off are poisonous to many insects. When the insects eat the poison, it destroys the walls of their stomachs. Unable to nourish themselves, they soon die.

A crop duster spreads a powder made of bacterial wastes on a farmer's field.

To make the germ-based insect poison, workers grow large amounts of bacteria in tanks. When the germs start releasing the poison, the workers dry them out, creating a powder. The powder is then sprayed on crops. The powder is harmless to the crops, but it kills the insect pests. An important advantage of this method is that the powder is also harmless to the soil and to animals and people.

Oil-Eating Germs Unleashed

In addition to getting rid of raw sewage and insect pests, germs can be used to clean up oil spills. In the past fifty years, oil tanker trucks and ships have leaked huge amounts of oil into fields, rivers, and oceans. The spilled oil pollutes these areas and kills many plants and animals. One of the worst of these disasters occurred in 1989. The tanker ship *Exxon Valdez* hit a reef in Prince William Sound in Alaska. Millions of gallons of oil spread into the sea and over beaches for hundreds of miles, killing thousands of fish, birds, and other creatures.

Oil spills, which harm birds and fish, can be cleaned up with bacteria.

The *Exxon Valdez* accident resulted in the first major use of germs to clean up an oil spill. Scientists put large amounts of special oil-eating bacteria in sacks of dirt. They placed some of the sacks on the bottom of Prince William Sound. Then they put the other sacks on the polluted beaches. As the days and weeks went by, the action of the waves and tides spread the dirt over much of the region. The bacteria in the dirt began eating and digesting the oil.

After two years, the scientists checked to see how well the germs had done their job. The researchers

A researcher tries to find a way to produce bacteria that will consume oil faster.

were pleased. They saw that, when used along with standard cleanup methods, the bacteria worked well. Since that time, this same type of germ has been used to combat several other oil spills.

The only problem with the method is that it works very slowly. To clean up oil from a typical spill may take two to five years. Scientists are presently trying to develop a bacterium that eats oil faster.

There is little doubt that this effort will succeed. Scientists look forward to this and many other new uses for germs. In the future, experts say, germs will create new food sources for starving populations. And good germs will make medicines to fight bad germs and help conquer disease. The tiniest, simplest living things—germs—will continue to make life better for the most complex living things—human beings.

Glossary

algae: A class of plantlike living things that includes microscopic germs that absorb sunlight and carbon dioxide and give off oxygen.

antibodies: Tiny particles created by the body to attack and destroy germs and other foreign objects entering the body.

bacteria: Small germs that live almost everywhere in nature and reproduce by splitting in half.

epidemic: A large outbreak of a disease that infects hundreds, thousands, or even millions of animals or people.

epidemiologist: A doctor who specializes in tracking down the source of a disease and then trying to keep that disease from spreading. Epidemiologists are often called "disease detectives."

fungi: A class of plantlike living things that includes microscopic germs that cause dead plants and animals to decay.

protozoa: Large germs that live in water or other liquids. Protozoa have some internal structure, including a nucleus in the center.

reproduce: To multiply or have offspring.

sludge: The solid portion of the waste materials people flush down their toilets.

spores: Tiny particles given off by fungi during reproduction. Each spore grows into a new fungus.

viruses: Extremely tiny germs that invade plant, animal, and human cells and sometimes cause serious diseases.

For Further Exploration

Molly Bang, *Chattanooga Sludge: Cleaning Toxic Sludge from Chattanooga Creek*. New York: Harcourt Brace, 1996. Written for basic readers, this is the story of how a scientist cleaned up a polluted waterway using simple bacteria. Highly recommended.

Melvin Berger, *Germs Make Me Sick*. New York: HarperCollins, 1995. Tells how bacteria and viruses spread infection and how the human body fights back. A very good book.

Mark P. Friedlander, *Outbreak: Disease Detectives at Work*. Minneapolis: Lerner, 2000. A fact-filled volume explaining how scientists and doctors trace the source of disease epidemics and stop them from spreading.

Robert Snedden and Steve Parker, *Yuck! A Big Book of Little Horrors*. New York: Simon and Schuster, 1996. Contains numerous large, colorful magnified pictures of germs (and other microscopic creatures, such as dust mites). Each picture has a clearly written, accurate explanation of the "little horror."

Index

Africa, 14, 21–23
AIDS, 4
Alaska, 39–41
algae, 9–10, 26
antibodies
   diseases and, 17
   vaccines and, 19–21

bacteria, 6–8
   bubonic plague and, 14
   cheeses and, 33
   food of, 26
   insect pests and, 37–38
   oil spills, 38, 40
   sludge and, 36–37
   vitamins and, 32
Black Death, 14
bubonic plague. *See* Black
   Death

carbon, 27
carbon dioxide, 9–10
cheeses, 33
chicken pox, 4
colds, 17

death, 26–27
decay, 26–27
digestion, 29–30
diseases, 4
   fighting, 17
   identifying causes of,
     15–17
   preventing, 19–21

protozoa and, 13, 14,
   21–23
viruses and, 13–14
waste products of, 17

epidemics, 4
epidemiologist, 15
Exxon Valdez (oil tanker),
   39–41

fish, 10
fleas, 14
food
   algae and, 9–10
   of bacteria, 26
   digestion of, 29–30
   of fungi, 8, 26
   helpful germs and, 24,
     26, 28, 33, 35
   insect pests and, 37–38
food chain, 26
fuel, 37
fungi, 8–9, 26

germs
   helpful
     digestion and, 29–30
     food and, 24, 26, 28,
       33, 35
     pumping of blood and,
       30–32
     sewage treatment and,
       35–37
     vitamins and, 32
   number of, 28

grape juice, 33

habitats, 4
  of algae, 9
  of bacteria, 7–8
  of protozoa, 13, 21, 23
  of viruses, 13
  of yeast, 8–9
harmful germs. *See*
  diseases
harmless germs. *See*
  germs, helpful
heart, 30–32

influenza, 14
insects, 37–38
intestines, 29–30, 32

lyme disease, 4

malaria, 13
measles, 4
methane, 37
microscopes, 4
  bacteria and, 6
  diseases and, 15
  viruses and, 13
milk, 33
mushrooms, 8

nitrogen, 24, 26, 27
nucleus, 13

oil spills, 38–41
oxygen, 10

plants, 24, 26, 27
poisons, 37
pollution
  oil spills, 38–41
  poisons, 37

sludge, 35–37
Prince William Sound,
  39–41
protozoa, 10, 13, 14, 21–23

reproduction
  of bacteria, 6–7
  of fungi, 8
  of protozoa, 13
  of viruses, 13

sewage, 35–37
shapes
  of bacteria, 6
  of fungi, 8
  of viruses, 13
sizes
  of bacteria, 6
  of fungi, 8
  of helpful germs, 28
  of protozoa, 10–11
  of viruses, 13
sleeping sickness
  causes of, 13, 14
  fighting, 21–23
  symptoms of, 17
sludge, 35–37
spores, 8

toxins, 17

Uganda, 21–23

vaccines, 19–21
viruses, 13, 14
vitamins, 32

wines, 33

yeasts, 8–9, 33

Picture Credits

Cover photo: Geoff Tompkinson/Science Photo Library/Photo Researchers, Inc.

About the Author

In addition to his acclaimed volumes on ancient civilizations, historian Don Nardo has published several studies of modern scientific discoveries and phenomena. Among these are *The Extinction of the Dinosaurs, Vaccines,* and a biography of Charles Darwin, who advanced the modern theory of evolution. Mr. Nardo lives with his wife, Christine, in Massachusetts.